# *LILACS AND LAUGHTER*

BY

JANIS WALKER

AUTHOR OF

ALLELUIA! A GOSPEL DIARY

Books by Janis Walker

ALLELUIA! A GOSPEL DIARY

FIRST READING: A DIARY

HALLELUJAH! A PSALM RESPONSE DIARY

SECOND READING: A DIARY

A TRIP TO GRACE

SHEPHERDS

MYSTERY!

MYSTICS AND MASHED POTATOES

TO SEE THE KING

LILACS AND LAUGHTER

# LILACS AND LAUGHTER

BY

JANIS WALKER

PALLIUM PRESS

Scripture quotations marked NRSV are from The New Revised Standard Version Bible, copyright 1989, Division of Christian Education of the National Council of Churches of Christ in the United States of America.

Scripture quotations marked KJV are from the The King James Version of the Bible.

Every effort has been made to insure accuracy of text and quotations, and any errors or omissions brought to our attention will be corrected in future editions.

SECOND PRINTING 2022

Pallium Press, P.O. Box 60910, Palo Alto, CA 94306-0910
We regret that Pallium Press cannot accept or return unsolicited manuscripts.

## Check for new titles by Janis Walker at www.palliumpress.com

## Pallium Press books are available at www.Amazon.com, www.BarnesandNoble.com, or at your favorite local independent bookstore.

cover photos: Terry Walker
cover design: Janis Walker

### Copyright © 2022 by Janis Walker

All rights reserved. No part of this book may be reproduced, transmitted, stored in a retrieval system, or otherwise copied by any means whether electrical, mechanical, optical, or recording without the express written consent of Pallium Press, except for brief excerpts as part of reviews as permitted under the 1976 United States Copyright Act.

Printed in the United States of America.

ISBN 978-0-9991260-0-4

for

Lydia and Laura,

my grandmothers

and

for Ara,

my granddaughter

Acknowledgements

Thank you to Terry and Christopher and Zuli and Ara.
I love you all so much.

Special thanks to Rosemary for her persistent encouragement.

Thank you to "The Eleven," without whom ….

A.M.D.G.

March 25, 2022

The Annunciation of the Lord
to
the Blessed Virgin Mary

## ST. LUKE, LILACS, AND LAMBETH

This goes back to 1988, a very big year.

In March, my father died, so there was a trip to San Angelo, Texas. There was a wonderful Methodist minister, a military chaplain, who officiated at this brief service. Later, I wrote to the chaplain and he answered with so much care and understanding.

In the summer, Terry and I traveled with a small group to England to attend the opening Sung Eucharist of the Lambeth Conference at Canterbury Cathedral. As I recall, a Roman Catholic Cardinal was also in attendance.

Later in the summer, Terry and Christopher and I traveled to Halifax, Nova Scotia, for me to attend an Order of St. Luke the Physician Conference. Terry and Christopher explored Halifax while I attended the conference This is where I first encountered LILACS. They were in full bloom and were glorious!

Then we three flew to Prince Edward Island to see the Anne of Green Gables house. Our inn was right across the meadow, so I could go back and forth a few wonderful times. So grateful to the Canadian Park Service for keeping Anne's house so lovingly maintained. More LILACS in bloom on P.E.I.!

After being in Canada and enjoying LILACS everywhere, we went to Grafton, the village in Vermont we had visited in past years. Near our inn, there is a really cold pond where I love to swim. It was great to have Christopher, then age thirteen, with us. In past years, we had gone to Grafton while Christopher was at Boy Scout camp.

From Vermont we went to Cambridge, Massachusetts, and then on to Madison, Wisconsin, and finally back to California. Back to work for Terry. Back to school for Christopher and back to seminary for me.

## BACK FROM THE SEA

Some years ago, Terry and I had several wonderful days to spend at the ocean at Pajaro Dunes.

Even though it was a crisp November week-end, I still couldn't wait to run down to the beach.

Leaving the suitcases, instead of giving in to my usual mode of first unpacking, I headed down the steps, across the sand, and into the wet part of the beach, where the waves were just brushing the sand.

WHAT?!

I was startled to experience the rush of waves. Backing back, I felt a little disoriented.

Even scarier, I looked down and noticed my right water sandal was missing.

This was really scary, since I needed both special sandals to make it back to our week-end retreat home.

Praying quickly, I asked God to send the right sandal back.

Whoosh!

There it was.

Quickly, I sprang forward and grabbed it from the wet sand. Considerably shaken, I put it back on.

In all the previous visits to the ocean, I had never encountered the intensity of the winds and waves. Still, I was safe.

THANK GOD!

My husband jokingly said, "God isn't ready for you yet. Even your sandal came back."

## CIRCUITS AND SOUL

For many years, Terry attended the ISSCC (International Solid State Circuits Conference) in San Francisco. It was over a period of a few days, usually in January. It was truly international, with scientists and engineers attending from all over the world.

Occasionally, on one of the days, I went with Terry and did other things during his time at the conference. The meetings were in the Marriot near Union Square.

Usually, I would carry along Valentines to send to "the aunts." Terry's mother, Doris, was one of six sisters, so it was a lot of fun for me to have aunts, even if they were in Texas.

Terry would take the long, long escalator to the conference area and I would head for the little coffee stand in the lobby. Armed with a nice, strong coffee, I would then go to the (at that time) lovely area upstairs with an indoor fountain and murals. Then I spread out the Valentines and had fun writing little notes, addressing and stamping them.

There were a few places of interest near the hotel, such as a lovely, old-fashioned hardware store and a Container Store which I liked to visit.

Then, I walked to the noon Mass around the corner at St. Patrick's Church. Oh, my, was there ever a SURPRISE one time at that Mass!

At the prayers of the people, the woman leading the prayers calmly stated, "At this Mass, we have been asked to pray for the soul of King Henry VIII of England."

Even now, decades later, I marvel at that particular prayer at that particular time. God's timing is always perfect and often, to us, mysterious.

After Mass, Terry and I met for a small lunch in the hotel. Then Terry went back to the conference.

In the afternoon, I walked a bit, sometimes to Union Square, and then went to the pool in the hotel. For a nominal fee, I enjoyed a refreshing lap swim.

Before heading back home, Terry and I would have a lovely dinner, usually in or near the hotel.

A day away.

Circuits and soul.

## A WEEK OF HEALING

Some years ago, on a Sunday, we had dinner with a friend from Stanford graduate school days in the 1970's. He was here on business from Chicago.

There were four couples who had met for weekly Bible study and prayer. We met in each other's homes in Escondido Village on campus.

This particular friend, Jim, had graduated and moved back to the Midwest with his wife and two sons. Shortly after returning, their third son was born with Down's Syndrome.

Then Jim went to the doctor and was diagnosed with a very serious disease. The doctors did exploratory surgery and found that the disease had spread. There was no hope.

Really? What happened then?

Leaders from Jim's church came to pray for him. Just like in the Bible.

"Are any among you sick? They should call for the elders of the church and have them pray over them, anointing them with oil in the name of the Lord. The prayer of faith will save the sick, and the Lord will raise them up; and anyone who has committed sins will be forgiven. Therefore confess your sins to one another, and pray for one another, so that you may be healed. The prayer of the righteous is powerful and effective (James 5, 14-16)."

Jim was healed!

That was over thirty years ago.

Yesterday, Saturday, there was Mass with Anointing at our parish. Having had an ultrasound test on Friday and being scheduled to see a surgeon soon, I was thankful for this service. I believe that many times God heals us when we don't even know what is wrong.

A mystery.

Healing has always been a mystery.

Stories like Jim's give us hope to believe that God is the God of the impossible.

Now, 25 years after that ultrasound test and surgery, I am still alive.

ALLELUIA!

## THEY DON'T KNOW WHAT WE KNOW

A couple of weeks ago, Kay did what is usually called dying.

She was almost 100 years old and just as glamorous as always. Her hair was beautiful and she had lovely manicured, polished nails.

We met in a prayer group, which, at one time, included women from their thirties to their nineties.

Kay had been a faithful intercessor for a young medical student who had been in a coma for a long time.

Chris, Kay's daughter, told us of something wonderful that happened before Kay left.

Kay apparently was receiving glimpses into heaven and was so happy.

She was talking with friends she knew who had gone before her.

Then, referring to the people standing near her in her hospital room, she spoke to her friends who were already "there," saying, "They don't know what we know!"

Indeed, we don't. But, hearing this story gave us all such joy and anticipation. We don't know now, but we shall know.

## WAITING

Decades ago, a wise, older Episcopal priest told me he had a word of the Lord for me.

Very curious, I waited for this word.

It was from Psalm 37.

Those who " ... wait on the Lord, they shall inherit the earth (Psalm 37, 9 KJV)."

The fulfillment of this particular promise has not yet come to pass.

I still wait.

Until that time, what do I do?

Continue to work and to trust.

"Rest in the Lord, and wait patiently for him …. (Psalm 37, 7 KJV)."

## THANK GOD FOR THE PAIN

The pain I was experiencing led me to seek medical help.

Because of two quick-witted nurses, I am still alive. The doctor was out of town, but the nurses decided the doctor would have wanted me to go immediately for an ultrasound.

The ultrasound, while showing that the source of the pain was temporary, also showed a cyst that was not temporary. Yes, there will be more surgery, but yes, I will be alive.

## DISCOUNTS AT DRAEGER'S

Once in a while, I still enjoy shopping at Draeger's, even if it is pricey.

We were living in Escondido Village on the Stanford campus when I first heard of Draeger's. A British friend from the Bible study, Freda, told me about Draeger's Supermarket. She particularly liked their huge cheese selection.

This day at Draeger's, however, was different.

It seemed that nearly everything on my short list was on sale!

This was one of the many ways the Lord cared for me tenderly before, during, and after my surgery.

Little signs of love and understanding.

## RECOGNIZE AND RISE ABOVE

Just because something is obvious doesn't mean I have to dwell on it.

God can help me rise above whatever it is.

## SPEECH OR SILENCE?

There was something I had a lot of trouble keeping quiet about.

It went back many years and I still felt agitated.

Having done all that was possible for me to do in the way of releasing, forgiving, etc. I was still bothered if I thought about it.

Today, Ann, my wise friend and one of my two sponsors when I was received into the Catholic Church, phoned me.

After hearing her news, I found myself again referring, obliquely, to this old situation.

The Lord is asking me again and again to keep silent about this matter.

It does no good to refer to it.

In the silence, the Lord will meet me.

In the silence, the Lord will heal me.

In silence the Lord is healing me.

## IS MY COMPUTER JEWISH?

Every time I wrote the word "sabbath," the computer would

automatically change it to "Sabbath."

I am a Catholic with Jewish ancestry, having a Cohen great-grandmother, on Mother's side, in my family tree.

I never met Marie Cohen Meier. She was only thirty-three when she died.

Still, I look at her photograph and think of her.

We cherish our Jewish friends.

The computer seems to know this!

## BELIEVE!

If you are praying and feeling discouraged, take heart!

BELIEVE (because it's true) that the Lord is listening to your prayers and is acting on your behalf and on the behalf of those for whom you are praying.

This morning, I was returning from Mass, the grocery store, the doughnut shop (hey, I don't go there very often), the garden center, a coffee house (where I enjoyed the previously mentioned doughnut), and then headed home.

As I drove by a drug store, I decided to stop for a quick purchase.

The store was out of this product, but what happened next was clearly the reason I had stopped.

Out of the sound system came the following words of a song, "I believe in redemption. There is hope for every soul."

That was it.

Silence.

I left, without my intended purchase, but very happy.

How precise is God's timing!

I was in that store at the exact time that song was being played.

When we pray for people, we have NO idea how and when and where God will speak to them.

God is infinitely creative and may even speak through the lyrics of piped in music in a pharmacy.

## A PHONE CALL AND A PROMISE

It was still early morning when the phone rang.

It was a friend from out of state who had a verse of Scripture to share with me.

The verse was Leviticus 26, 13, about the Lord's promise of freedom! " … I have broken the bonds of your yoke, and made you go upright (Leviticus 26, 13b KJV)"

This verse energized me to meet the day. It has been gray and humid for quite a while following all the fires in California. As I drove away, singing, the sky cleared and became blue again. The sun shone!

## INTERIOR MISTRAL

What is happening?

Everything is blowing around and shaking up my little world.

Thank you, Lord Jesus, that you are still in control of the winds and the waves and that you will lead me safely Home.

## RESTORATION

Drilling and filling!

Our former dentist, now retired, had a whimsical way of describing the upcoming dental procedure. "We're going to restore the area."

God restores many areas in our lives. Yes, there is drilling and filling.

God drills out what is decayed and fill in the empty spaces with "gold."

## THIRD BLOOMING

We've become excited about the second blooming of the wisteria on the fence.. If, after the first blooming, it is carefully pruned, it will actually bloom again. The second blooms are even more purply than the first.

A third blooming, however, had not occurred until this year. This year, the Lord knew I need extra reassurance.

So, a third blooming.

## CHERRY AMES AND THE CHURCH

As a child and teenager, I loved to read the Cherry Ames nurse stories. I did not know then that the Lord would call me to another kind of healing.

The Lord would call me to a kind of healing in HIS BODY.

The CHURCH.

Jesus is the head of the Church. We are members of his Body.

We need healing.

### A POWERFUL PRAYER

Although I was not a Catholic at the time, I prayed a particular prayer which is so powerful. One time, I was to drive some Catholic ladies to a pro-life meeting in San Francisco.

I felt sick and decided to pray this prayer. It was truly amazing! I recovered quickly and drove the ladies to a wonderful meeting we all enjoyed.

The prayer is,

"In obedience to the Immaculate Conception, I command you, every unclean spirit to depart: cease your attacks on us, our family, business, surroundings, and on those for whom we pray. In the Name of Jesus, I command you into the deep pit."

Now, make the sign of the cross three times. This prayer has ecclesiastical approval. There are prayer cards with this prayer available from Our Lady of Guadalupe Abbey. Lafayette, Oregon 97127.

### AN ADVENT SURPRISE

Years ago, there were television ads about a store that was collecting Christmas toys for children who are in foster care. So, on the way to the fish market, I stopped to buy for a few things for these children. I bought a huge box of crayons. a coloring book about botanical gardens, and an adorable soft stuffed toy cat.

At the cash register, I was surprised when the clerk named an amount obviously under the amount I owed. He said he had heard about the collection for the foster children and he wanted to contribute the toy cat!

And, if that weren't enough, the lady behind me in line had a stuffed toy dog she was giving to the children. The clerk paid for that too and put in my sack to deliver to the store!

I was stunned by this kindness. This area can be so competitive and cynical. And yet, today, Jesus touched the hearts of strangers to give to the children.

## FITTED AND FILLED

Psalm 71.

Look it up.

Read it prayerfully, very, very slowly.

You will understand.

## ALREADY DONE!

Many years ago, we had a lot of boxes outside in a PODS (Portable on Demand Storage). This was a great help while we were having some work done inside the house.

Then, I began to fret about a file cabinet that had been in my study. Useful, but not pretty. Really didn't want it back, but did not want to throw away the contents.

Lo and behold, when I mentioned this dilemma to Terry, he made my day by saying that he had already placed the contents of that cabinet in another larger file cabinet in another room.

I really need help in the matter of what to keep and what to get rid of, whether it material or emotional.

## BEGINNING OF THE WEEK

This was the first two days of the 2009 Week of Prayer for Christian Unity

Sunday -- phoned Carlton and Sharon. Carlton (The Rev. Dr. Carlton Young) was our Clinical Pastoral Education supervisor in the summer of 1994). Sharon was one of the other summer interns, along with Anna, Juanita, Cynthia, Dorothy, and me. We were all Christians, but from different denominations. This was before I became Roman Catholic.

Monday -- noticed a crowd at the Russian Orthodox Church across the street from the YMCA where I swim. Then I chatted with Larisa, a Russian, at the front desk of the Y.

Well, it is now 2022, as I proofread this manuscript. I'm not sure what went on the rest of that particular Week of Prayer. In past years, there were services at various churches in nearby cities, to which all were invited.

## TANGLED PRAYERS

This morning, I took a few moments of quiet to pray the Glorious Mysteries of the rosary. Two rosaries had become entangled on the table and I tried, without success, to disentangle them before praying.

Finally, I just began to pray. After all, the rosary is a prayer. The prayer itself is what is important. A little later, I noticed the rosary beads were untangled.

How many times do we hesitate to pray, thinking that various aspects of our lives, or the lives of those for whom we pray, need to be just so before we can pray?

God is delighted when we just begin where we are. God will gently take care of the tangles.

## RAZED AND RAISED

When we feel annihilated and razed by the troubles of this life, we need to remember where our true life is situated.

Our true life is safe.

WE are safe.

Our true life is with Christ. We have been raised with Christ. We are already in the heavenly realm (Ephesians 2, 6).

## CHAIR

There is a nearby Catholic church where I sometimes go for the sacrament of reconciliation. This church has the traditional confession boxes with kneelers.

For the last few weeks, I have had knee problems. Having completely forgotten about the question of the kneeler, I entered the confessional.

There was the kneeler AND a chair! I was so thankful. The Lord had taken care of the situation even before I thought of it.

## RETREAT HOUSE

A friend who just moved across the country and I were chatting on the phone. We were commiserating about various frustrations and all the noise in our respective cities.

There is the desire to be quiet, to be still, and to stay away from the noise and aggression of our world.

A place of retreat and renewal is always available.

All we need to do is to realize that we are in the heart of God.

This is a place of security, peace, and healing.

## CHECK IT THROUGH!

It is possible to travel light.

It's possible to travel so light that we just take one carry-on piece of luggage with us and perhaps not even take any baggage that needs to be checked through to our final destination.

We know a man who doesn't even pack, but waits and buys what is needed upon arrival at destination!

What about carry-on baggage that is a burden?

Yes, it's possible to continue to carry it, but why? Why not check it through and be free of its burden?

Final destination.

Where is my final destination?

It is to be forever with the LORD GOD!

What do I need to check through to my final destination? I don't need to be lugging around the baggage of the past. I don't need to be burdened with old baggage of past injuries and grievances.

I don't need to carry it with me everywhere.

The Lord wants this baggage, so I can be free.

The Lord, who knows what to do, will do a mighty work of healing and purification.

I will be free at last.

Thank God Almighty.

I am free at last!

## BABY BIRDS IN THE WISTERIA

We have a birdhouse in the wisteria where a little bird family lives. It has been so sweet to see the busy parents going to and from their nest, bringing food for their little ones.

## GOD'S PARSLEY

Parsley!

That dark green curly stuff some people like to use to decorate salads, etc. It's also useful to cover up culinary mistakes! Just sprinkle the goof with a bit of parsley.

Some people are like parsley. They are very humble.

They do not mind being misunderstood. They are not doormats, but they are willing for God to use them to cover the mistakes of others.

They understand that God always has the final word.

## WOUNDS

So often, I sin out of my wounds and my need to defend myself.

As we learn, little by little to respond in God's way, we will become stronger and more confident. We will not be driven to defend ourselves and to try to make sure we have our own way.

Lord Jesus, we all have wounds. We have wounds from the past when we were hurt or unjustly treated. Help us to respond to the "workbook exercises" of this life in your way. Thank you for the healing and joy you have in store for us.

## THE BLUE CASTLE

Many years after our trip to Prince Edward Island in Canada, I came across another book by L.M Montgomery, the author of the well-known Anne of Green Gables books.

The Blue Castle was published in 1926 and is quite different from the Anne stories.

This is a story of great redemption, but you have to be patient, stay with it, and work for the "happy" ending.

A major character in the book, the mysterious John Foster, author of many nature books, was very wise. He wrote that "Fear is the original sin. Almost all the evil in the world has its origin in the fact that someone is afraid of something."

Valancy, the "heroine" of this most unusual book, remembered this saying of John Foster, and was set free from her fear and began her new, transformed life,

## A LITTLE BARNABAS BIRD

I was outside listening to the homily for today's Mass on Relevant Radio. Today is June 11, St. Barnabas, whose name, in Greek, means "son of encouragement."

Glancing up, I saw a little hummingbird swoop over to the hummingbird feeder for a little sip of nectar. I have always felt uplifted when I see hummingbirds and hear the amazing flutter of their strong little wings.

Right now, with all the flowers in bloom, they don't need the extra feeder, so I was especially happy to see this little bird. Even when we don't have a human friend to encourage us at a particular moment, God knows how to send little messengers of hope and encouragement.

## GRADUATION

On this bright June day, when so many are graduating, I was feeling a bit low and went to spend an hour in a Blessed Sacrament Chapel. This is a very simple chapel, full of air and light.

## JESUS!

Jesus on the Cross.

Jesus, on your "Graduation Day," you did not have people wishing you well and saying "Congratulations." You were mocked, tortured, spat upon, and nailed to a Cross to die.

Instead of an academic robe, you were clothed in a purple cloak intended to mock your royalty.

Instead of being handed a diploma, you were given a Cross to carry.

Instead of hearing the applause of well-wishers, you heard angry cries of "Crucify him."

As you hung on the Cross, when you knew that your work of redemption was complete, you said, "It is finished." (John 19, 20)

Lord Jesus, help us to see our disappointments in this life from your perspective. Help us to believe, with all our heart, that you love us and that you are working out every detail of our lives and the lives of those we love in the very best way.

## YOUNG CATHOLICS TO THE MAX IN THE DELI

After my time in the chapel, I drove to a nearby deli to have a coffee and to sit on a bench in the sunshine.

A young school boy with a rosary was ahead of me in the line. His shirt was something else! It read, "LIVE HOLY OR DIE." I commented on it and asked where he went to school. It was a public school.

Then, outside, I noticed that he was with two other boys. One of them had a shirt with a picture of beloved Pope John Paul II and the inscription, "CHRIST OUR HOPE."

I thanked the three boys for being willing to acknowledge their faith in public and asked them to pray for someone I was concerned about. I drove away marveling at God's goodness to reassure me that there are still disciples in this world.

## GREAT BOOKS AND JULY 4

We were at a July 4 potluck some years ago at the home of friends. This group gets together once a year for this event.

A woman at the event was telling of her husband when he graduated from college. His mother offered him a choice of gifts. Either he could have a special watch or a set of the Great Books. He chose the watch and for years wished he had chosen the Great Books instead.

Well, we had a set of Great Books and wanted to free up that space in living room. I told her that if they would come and get the books for free, that would be great!

They were happy to get the books and we were happy to get the space back.

What happened to that empty space in our living room?

GIANNA happened!

Noticing an after-Christmas sale in a children's catalog, I ordered a white lamb, not knowing how large it would be.

A HUGE package was delivered to our front door!

Oh, no. What IS this?

Well, it was a very realistic-looking full-size SHEEP!

The good news is that Gianna fits perfectly into the space left by the bookcase containing the Great Books.

## ADVENT DIARY

November 29, 2009

Mass at Mission Santa Clara today with priest from Africa presiding. Little purple yarns were distributed after Mass to remind us that Advent is a holy season.

Lovely lunch after Mass with Terry at Frankie, Johnnie, and Luigi Too. Great Italian food, especially lasagna.

I want to learn to be as quiet as possible this Advent.

I'm very weary with trying to reach out to those who seem not to care. On a walk this afternoon I smiled and said "hello" to a passing couple. The man grudgingly and unsmiling looked very briefly at me and said "hello."

Lord Jesus, please help me to know how to live here. Tell me when to reach out and speak to others and when to be silent.

## HONEST LUNGS

Honest to God and honest to YOU!

If you can live and speak the truth, you are able to breathe.

If you have to pretend, you cannot breathe. You suffocate. You are not being true to God or to yourself.

Speak the truth to God and to yourself.

Breathe!

## THERE THEY ARE AGAIN!

How could I have been so frightened or threatened?

Every time I saw these people, I wanted to disappear. They would appear at various places and I would freeze.

They were the parents of one of our son's classmates many years ago. I am not sure why, but every time I saw them, I wanted to run for the hills.

Only now do I realize what an opportunity I may have missed. Instead of fleeing, why could I not have been more adventurous and at least have tried to get to know them better?

Obviously, we cannot be close friends with everyone.

Obviously, we are also to honor our innermost sense of caution and discernment.

However, some people are diamond in the rough and are potentially very good friends.

## THE DENTIST, THE DANCER, AND THE DIVER

Not so scary after all!

I had been dreading a social event for some time. It was a small birthday gathering for someone I did not know very well. He was a former colleague of my husband at Stanford.

Surprise!

Over the course of the evening, the other three women at the event and I really enjoyed getting to know one another.

Who could have guessed that the glamorous blonde who arrived in a very expensive sports car was a retired dentist? Who could have guessed that the lovely, dignified, very quiet woman was a dance instructor? Who could have guessed that the beautiful, mysteriously silent woman across the table was a passionate scuba diver and a grandmother?

This evening overturned all my previous fears and expectations!

It was lots of fun.

## MOTHER AND "FATIMA"

Judy, my sister traveled all over the world when she worked for the Princess cruise line. Once, after being in Portugal, she brought a small, lovely statue of Our Lady of Fatima to our mother, a Texas Methodist.

Mother referred to the statue as "Fatima." My sister tried to say, "Mother, this is a statue of the Blessed Virgin Mary. This is how she looked when she appeared in Portugal as Our Lady of Fatima.

Mother would indignantly reply, "Her name is FATIMA! It says so right there on the statue."

### ASH WEDNESDAY 2010

This was one of the most unusual Ash Wednesdays I have ever experienced. Thinking of it is still exhausting.

It began as cold, foggy, gray morning. Fortunately, I had already made my cup of coffee, because abruptly the electricity went off. No lights. No heat.

What was going on??

I had planned to be at the noon Ash Wednesday service in our parish, but was advised not to go there, because all the traffic lights were not working.

Also, I had planned, later in the afternoon to meet a friend for coffee after her doctor's appointment. That was cancelled because there was no electricity in the doctor's office and the phone lines did not work, either.

So, I ventured out to Mass at a closer church. Sitting at the back, someone tapped my shoulder. It was Ann, my confirmation sponsor, and her son. So, I went up front to sit with them.

This led to my assisting with the imposition of ashes. Such a privilege as person after person came up and I made the sign of the Cross on their forehead with the ashes, saying, "Turn away from sin and be faithful to the Gospel."

At Mass I learned more about why the electricity was out.

A small, private plane had run into some kind of power tower (my technical vocabulary is limited). All three people aboard were killed.

The plane landed into a street in East Palo Alto. A nearby home housed a day care center with little children present. Miraculously, no one was hurt.

Walking outside the church after Mass, I was greeted with the most beautiful day.

Sunshine!

It felt very much like spring.

More bad news.

It turned out that the three people who had died in the plane crash were from Tesla, a nearby company. They had planned to fly to Caltech in Pasadena where my son is and to conduct job interviews.

How fragile is this life.

All these years later, I am still overwhelmed when I remember that day.

Lord, have mercy. Christ, have mercy. Lord, Have mercy. Help us to turn away from sin and be faithful to the Gospel.

## THE BLACK TEAPOT

All the way to Cambridge, England, to see a black teapot?!

Well, yes.

We were in England for many reasons, but seeing this exhibit, including the teapot was still important to me.

It was the teapot of a holy Anglican priest. His life and ministry inspired me.

Charles Simeon.

## KNOTS

A friend once gave me a little booklet called "Mary, Undoer of Knots."

This is a novena to the Blessed Virgin Mary to ask her intercession in undoing the various puzzling, frustrating "knots" in our lives, situations which seem to have no solution.

So, with my rosary, I began to pray. The novena consists of praying the rosary as well as a few short prayers each day.

Another knot! This was a knot IN my rosary, alas.

This particular rosary, a beautiful pearl rosary given to me by a friend, Beth, had somehow become knotted.

At first, I tried to undo the knot in the rosary, with no success. Then I simply began to pray. As I finished the last of the prayers, I noticed that the rosary had become completely unknotted!

A lesson in beginning to pray as we are able and leave to God the untying of all the frustrating "knots" in our lives.

There is a beautiful painting of "Mary, Undoer of Knots."

Since 1700, this painting has been in Germany at St. Peter's Church in Perlack.

## CONFESSION AND WINGS

The Lord really has a sense of humor!

It was Friday at Mass. I had been to confession (the sacrament of reconciliation) the previous Saturday, but on Monday I had really blown it. I had already asked the Lord to forgive me, but really wanted to go the to the powerful and freeing sacrament of reconciliation.

So, during Mass on Friday, I prayed that the Lord would somehow provide an opportunity to go to confession before Saturday. It seemed unlikely. The presider at that particular Friday Mass usually has to leave immediately after Mass through the sacristy.

Surprise!

The priest went to the door to greet the people. I waited and was able to make my confession then and there!

Lord Jesus, thank you for the sense of having been given wings! Thank you for forgiving me. Thank you for the sacrament of reconciliation. Bless all priests who hear confessions.

## SILENCE IS SPEECH!

Silence.

I wish I could go back and say it differently.

Sometimes it's better to stay quiet and let the Lord sort it out.

Silence.

## TYRANNY OF LOW EXPECTATIONS

Today is Bastille Day, July 14!

Breaking free from prison.

Liberty!

There is another kind of freedom we still need.

Sometimes we do not realize that we are held captive by our ourselves.

We may have low expectations.

Life has been hard and we may have silently given up hope.

Lord Jesus, free us to be all that you want us to be.

Let us begin to live again!

ALLELUIA in advance!

### THE PHYSICIST, THE TONSILS, AND THE SURFER

An applied physics major, our son, Christopher, had come up from Caltech in Pasadena, for a tonsillectomy. Not a great experience for a young adult, but it had to be done.

He weathered the surgery which was performed at a same-day surgery center. Alas, after one week, however, we heard him banging on the wall in the middle of the night. He had begun bleeding!

Terry rushed him to the Emergency Room of the hospital and I followed in the other car. The problem seemed to be resolved and he was sent home.

Not so!

The bleeding resumed and so we raced back to the Emergency Room. This time, they kept him at the hospital until his doctor's office opened at 9:00 a.m. His doctor had to do another procedure.

Meanwhile, back at home, it was approaching Terry's birthday. Christopher wanted to prepare a special meal for his dad, even though he himself was still recovering from the two surgical procedures.

We went to the supermarket to purchase the ingredients. Christopher wanted a specific kind of cast iron skillet for the steak. This was a skillet we did not have.

We then drove downtown to Domus, a cooking store, to check on this kind of skillet. Christopher, unable to speak, wrote his message on a slate and held it up to the clerk.

With the afternoon evaporating and no skillet, he began to check on the internet for the skillet while I thumbed through the Yellow Pages. Within a few minutes, we both discovered that a nearby hardware store in our town carried this kind of skillet!

I phoned the store to ask them please to stay open a little bit longer and we drove over to purchase our prized skillet.

The dinner he prepared was phenomenal!

SO good!

It was a Lodge cast iron skillet, somehow difficult to get at that time.

After Christopher returned to southern California, I returned to the downtown cooking store for something else. The people there clearly remembered our previous visit!

Christopher, during his convalescence, had grown a beard, a reddish gold beard! He is a blond, but the beard was clearly reddish. The clerk, having heard about his surgery, asked about him. "He's going to be a physicist," I answered, "and he was getting over a tonsillectomy the time we were here looking for the skillet."

The clerk, clearly dazed, replied, "A physicist?! Man, I thought, with that beard, he was some kind of surfer dude."

## I SEE A LAMB

How completely irritating! We had just finished the design for the cover of my first book and I was so happy with the drawing of the lamb.

Others, however, seeing the lamb, thought it was a dog!

A dog?!

I was outraged. No one is going to call that lamb a dog.

Back to the drawing board, I guess.

Just one more detail to be ironed out before the book is released.

I still think that first drawing looks like a lamb.

## THE POPE AND THE AVOCADO

I had been to the nearby carwash and really splurged! I usually just get an exterior wash, but this time I had an interior cleaning as well.

When the car was ready, I hopped in and guess who was looking at me?

THE POPE!

The person cleaning the interior had unearthed a holy card of the Pope and placed it right where I could see it.

Another surprise!

On the seat of the passenger side was an avocado. An old avocado. I think my friend, Eleanor, had given it to me after Mass some time ago and it had rolled under the seat.

When you start cleaning, you never know what you will find!

## ROUTINE REVERENCE

As I was reading Isaiah 29, 13, I was startled to see the indictment about the reverence of God's people having become merely routine.

"Therefore, the Lord said … this people draw near me with their mouth, and with their lips do honor me, but have removed their heart far from me…. (Isaiah 29, 13a KJV)."

Lord Jesus, forgive us when we become routine and automatic in our worship. Forgive us for wounding your tender heart of love and grieving you. Have mercy on us. Let us draw near to you and be assured and reassured that you love us and you long to gather us into your arms.

## ONE LOVE

In great anguish over a seemingly irresolvable situation, I prayed and was led to a passage in *The Smiling Pope*, a collection of writings from Pope John Paul I. This was a quote from "Joy, Exquisite Love", a "letter" the Pope wrote to Saint Therese of Lisieux.

The sentence that helped me so much was, " … there are not many loves, but only one."

This is, of course, the love of Christ which expands to include all.

Dear Pope John Paul I, Papa Luciani, please pray for us.

## "BE STILL, MY SOUL"

Last Wednesday, I was enjoying an hour with the Lord before the Blessed Sacrament in a tiny chapel. I felt led to find and to the words from the hymn, "Be Still My Soul." I copied out the entire hymn and basked in the assurance it offers.

The next day, Thursday, I received a gift from a colleague from Clinical Pastoral Education days. It was a lovely Christmas card and also a CD of instrumental music from many hymns.

On Friday, Christmas Eve, I actually opened the CD and was stunned to discover the hymn "Be Still, My Soul" printed out in its entirety. All the words I had grown to love.

Something else! The background was a lovely blue sky with clouds. That was the background of my first book, ALLELUIA, A GOSPEL DIARY!

Lord Jesus, thank you for the overwhelming comfort this has brought me. You were with me in the chapel as I read and prayed the words of the hymn. You were with me when I opened my friend's gift. You were with me when I saw the very same words printed on the blue sky with clouds background. Thank you for reminding me that you are with me at every moment and that you have good planned for me. Please heal me of my fear. Alleluia! Alleluia!

## A PINK HIBISCUS OUT OF THE BLUE

Rather drearily and dutifully, I went out to take a walk.

Motion always helps!

Nothing terrible had happened. It was just one of those ordinary days in ordinary time.

All of a sudden, I spotted a blossom, a perfect blossom, on the sidewalk. What in the world?

It was a bright, happy pink hibiscus! There were no hibiscus bushes anywhere nearby.

Whatever the reason for its presence there, I felt lighter and happier. The Lord knew I needed a lift in my spirits that day and a perfect pink hibiscus was just the ticket.

## LOOK INTO HIS EYES

Praying the joyful mysteries of the rosary, I came to the fourth mystery, the presentation of the infant Jesus in the Temple in Jerusalem. The infant Jesus may have gazed into the eyes of the elderly Simeon, who had so long awaited the birth of the Messiah!

In the fifth mystery, the finding of Jesus, age twelve, in the Temple in Jerusalem, I pondered how Jesus may have looked into the eyes of the teachers of the law and also into the frantic, distraught eyes of Mary and Joseph.

Recently I heard something about the training of police officers. If an officer is seemingly cornered by someone with a gun, the officer is to look into the eyes of the other person. It is meant to establish contact, an acknowledgement of common humanity.

Lord Jesus, I gaze into your eyes on this day, this Lenten day, March 26, 2013. Help me to see your tender compassion and understanding. Please continue to heal me and to set me free from my fears and misconceptions.

## KNEELING IN NORDSTROM

Goodness, only Jesus and Helen could have pulled this off!

I just got off the phone with my friend Helen. Today is April 19, 2013, and we were praying for the situation in Boston.

Helen will tell me all about the Nordstrom event later. Apparently, she was in the café at Nordstrom and a young man knelt in prayer. Can't wait to hear the whole story. Wherever Helen goes, she lives the Gospel, and as St. Francis said, she sometimes uses words.

## FEEDING SNAILS

Meredith!

Meredith and her husband, Phil, were friends when we were living on the Stanford campus during graduate school days. We were in a Bible study and prayer group.

Meredith loved all of God's creatures and even kept a pet snail. Once, she even went to the garden center and asked, "What kind of food should I feed my snail?"

The astonished answer was, "Most people want to kill snails and YOU want to feed them?"

## ADVENT BUDS

Spring!

Today, December 3, 2013, I stopped by a little church where I love to be with Jesus in the Blessed Sacrament Chapel.

It's only the beginning of Advent and yet the pink magnolia tree already has its soft, grey little buds, the promise of spring. Blossoms will appear!

Lord Jesus, thank you for this reminder, in cold Advent, that you are preparing me for springtime. There will be blossoms, pink, fragrant blossoms on the little magnolia tree. Although I have waited for so long, there will also be blossoms in my life. Please help me to relax into your plan and your timing. You know what you are doing. I place all my trust in you. Thank you for the Holy Spirit who strengthens me to wait for spring.

## CLEANSING AND DIRECTION

Being in spiritual direction is a great privilege, but not all are able to have a director. There is, however, a strong element of spiritual direction in the sacrament of reconciliation.

There is a great sense of joy and release upon hearing the absolution. Our sins are forgiven. They are gone!

Now we are free to follow the path the Lord has directed us to follow!


## MY TROUSSEAU

I was busy making changes and corrections in <u>Second Reading, A Diary</u>. This was very tedious and I was getting frustrated and bored.

The Holy Spirit whispered, "This is part of your trousseau."

WHAT!

What is that supposed to mean?

I believe the Lord was reassuring me that this tedious work can be likened to a bride carefully preparing her trousseau and her hope chest. One day all these irritating earthly concerns will be over.

We will rejoice at the Wedding Supper of the Lamb. We will sing and dance throughout all eternity!

Lord Jesus, thank you for shifting my perspective. Please strengthen and energize me to keep on serving you as you have called me to serve you today.

### A SEAMLESS ALLELUIA!

On the way to Mass one day, I started singing, aloud, the eight-fold "Alleluia." I sang all the way to the church.

Surprise!

As I entered the church, the presider at Mass entered, singing "Alleluia"

"ALLELUIA"

### ONE LITTLE PREPOSITION

What a difference a preposition can make!

In this case, the prepositions were "with" and "on.

You've heard the saying, "God writes straight with crooked lines."

Well, I was reading the beautiful book, BENEDICTUS, by Pope Benedict XVI and came across a similar quote.

This time it was, "God writes straight over crooked lines."

OVER!

This resonates with me and reassures me.

No matter how the lines in my life became "crooked," whether from my own sins or the sins of others, GOD still has the final word and can and will write his perfect will for me OVER those crooked lines. Alleluia!

## FRIED CHICKEN IN THE MORNING DOWN BY THE RIVERSIDE

Glory be!

It is Sunday morning, the second Sunday of Advent, 2015. We are going to a later Mass, so I was luxuriating taking a bubble bath (geranium, rose, and lavender bath oils).

All of a sudden, there was the powerful fragrance of fresh hot fried chicken wafting through the open window accompanied by LOUD Gospel music. "Down by the Riverside!"

Now I'm dressed and ready for Mass, but this was such a FUN surprise. Fried chicken and Gospel music!

With the world and the country all in a terrorist dither, it was a sign to me that, of course, GOD wins and all will be well.

As it happens, the responsorial psalm today is Psalm 126, "The Reversal of Zion's Fortunes." "When the LORD restored the fortunes of Zion, we were like those who dream. Then our mouth was filled with laughter, and our tongue with shouts of joy; then it was said among the nations,' The LORD has done great things for them.' The LORD has done great things for us and we rejoiced (Psalm 126, 1-3 NRSV)."

Lord Jesus, thank you that you have the final word in our life and in the life of our poor suffering world. THANK YOU that we will rejoice forever with you. Alleluia!

## THE GREG, THE RED HAT, AND THE ALARM – JANUARY 1, 2016

It is February 28, 2022. I am proofreading and I honestly do not remember what this essay was to be about.

The "Greg" refers to the Gregorian in Rome.

Red hats refer to cardinals.

Other than that, I don't know. Oh, dear, I am curious. That's what comes of waiting too long to proofread!

## TIMING, TIMING, TIMING!

Recently, I have become more and more aware of the Lord's loving sovereignty in my life in the matter of guidance and timing.

Last Sunday, Laetare Sunday, we had hoped to be able to go to Mass at Mission Santa Clara. With all the wild rain, welcome and needed as it is, it seemed unlikely that we would be able to go.

Lo and behold, Sunday morning was bright, sunny, and beautiful. Off to the Mission! Along with many other people. Standing room only.

Eventually, I was given a place to sit. Terry found another place. We were not able to sit together, but still it was a joy to be at Mass at this special place. Right before Communion, Terry was with me in the line. Surprise!

And then another surprise. The person sitting next to me insisted Terry take his place. So, we did get to sit together after all.

It was lovely to see friends after Mass and to admire the blooming wisteria, so fragrant in the spring sunshine.

After one or two tries at finding a place to have lunch that was not super-crowded, we went back to Palo Alto. After a long wait, we were given a table at the back of the restaurant. Not at the window as hoped, but still a table.

The real treat came as we were about to leave. It turned out that the people at the next table had recognized us! The woman and her daughter had known us from Stanford days long ago.

All these "little" signs of the Lord's guidance and provision touched me very much. The Lord is truly watching over us and placing us where we are meant to be. Alleluia in advance.

## RECALCULATING! RECALCULATING!

The voice on the GPS was getting desperate. We were not following exactly the directions.

The next message was a firm voice, saying "RECALCULATING," and then giving new directions.

The Lord knows how to recalculate and how to re-direct us when we get off course. It will be OK.

## BEFORE THE BLESSED SACRAMENT

Recently I remembered two very powerful times of prayer before the Blessed Sacrament.

The first was in the spring of 1991 when I had my oral thesis defense at the seminary. Carol, a dear friend, told me she would not be present at the seminary, but would be praying for me before the Blessed Sacrament at Corpus Christi Monastery.

I was BEYOND grateful!

And then, some years later, Carol was giving a retreat in a nearby town. I was not there, but, all of a sudden, I knew I had to pray for Carol.

At that moment, I was near the Blessed Sacrament.

Later, I learned that Carol had misplaced her notes and the that Lord had led me to pray for her, not really knowing the details.

That is so wonderful. We do not need to know everything. We

just need to listen to the Lord and to obey the prompting of the Holy Spirit

ALLELUIA

## JERUSALEM!

It is a cold, bright and beautiful, but cold, spring morning. I was returning home after a quick run to the post office to send off two birthday gifts.

At the traffic light, I looked to the right and the driver in the car in the other lane was very animated, saying, "JERUSALEM!"

I smiled and answered back, "YES! JERUSALEM!"

The license plate for our car was JRSLM.

"Jerusalem, my happy home, When shall I come to thee? When shall my sorrows have an end? Thy joys when shall I see?" These are the first words of the song, "Jerusalem, My Happy Home."

## BRIDGE PRAYER AT THE DELI

Yesterday I was at a deli counter to get some roasted turkey to make sandwiches for Terry. A woman admired my Easter scarf (it was from the gift shop in the hotel where I had attended a conference in San Diego) with all the bright Easter eggs.

She confided that she was about to leave for San Francisco and would be driving across the Golden Gate bridge. She was very nervous about driving over the bridge.

I told her we had just been in San Francisco the day before and that it was lovely and the traffic was actually very light at that same time in the morning. We said good-bye and I promised prayers for a safe journey.

She was grateful and seemed relieved about the trip. This was such a tiny incident and yet it gave me courage to reach out to others.

### PRAYER-WORRIER OR PRAYER-WARRIOR?

Laughingly, I told a friend, "There is a saying that if you pray, why worry and if you worry, why pray?"

Yes, that's true, but I still do both.

I have a long way to go in the "Trusting God 101" class.

The good news is that this class lasts a lifetime.

The Holy Spirit, our teacher, is very patient with us and helps us to trust.

Long ago, I learned that, if something scary was coming up, I tried to pray, "Thank you, Lord, for this opportunity to trust you."

### "OVERPAST"

OVERPAST?

What in the world?

Years ago, this word, "overpast," came to mind and I could not shake it.

> "Come, my people, enter your chambers,
>   and shut your doors behind
>     you;
> hide yourselves for a little while
>   until the wrath is past (Isaiah 26, 20 NRSV)."

Overpast!

Where is that word?

I searched in my ancient, huge Strong's <u>Concordance</u>. It weighs a ton.

The translation in the <u>King James Version</u> for "past" is "overpast."

For some time, I have been led to more silence and seclusion in order to pray and to write.

This word "hide" was interesting.

Hide where?

Then today I was reading Psalm 32 in the Coverdale translation. "Thou art a place to hide me in; thou shalt preserve me from trouble; thou shalt compass me about with songs of deliverance."

The Lord knows how to "hide" us when we need to be hidden.

There is a time to be "out there."

There is also a time to be "hidden."

## TWO "VIOLENT!" VERBS

Well, maybe "violent" is too strong an adjective.

These verbs are still very strong.

"TORN!"

"In those days Jesus came from Nazareth of Galilee and was baptized by John in the Jordan. And just as he was coming up out of the water, he saw the heavens torn apart and the Spirit descending like a dove on him. And a voice came from heaven, 'You are my Son, the Beloved; with you I am well pleased (Mark 1, 9-11).'"

"ABANDONED!"

Mark 1, 16-20 describes Jesus by the Sea of Galilee. He saw the fishermen, Simon (Peter) and Andrew. "And Jesus said to them, 'Follow me and I will make you fish for people.' And immediately they left their nets and followed him (Mark 17, 18)."

However, the verbs "left" or "dropped," used in several translations, pales in comparison to the verb used in the <u>New American Bible</u>, which is "ABANDONED."

Andrew and Simon, who would be called Peter, saw Jesus, heard the call of Jesus and that was that! They ABANDONED their previous work and immediately followed Jesus.

CARRYING YOUR CROWN!

When you carry "your" cross, you are also carrying your future crown!

WHAT IS YOUR CREDIT SCORE?

There is quote somewhere that says you can really accomplish a LOT if you don't care WHO gets the credit.

God knows all you have done.

God knows.

GOD will reward you!

Well, I did find the quote.

"It is amazing what you can accomplish if you do not care who gets the credit."

This is a quote from President Harry Truman.

## THE NOTEBOOK

I have problems with looking back and rehashing past events over and over!

Do you ever have trouble with this too?

The Holy Spirit is beginning to set me free!

I had this idea of every day as a page in a notebook.

I could only look at the page for today.

No turning back to past pages because, guess what, there were NO past pages.

I am allowed only to live TODAY'S page!

## CARRYING TREES?

Exhausted.

Why?

As I prayed, the Lord seemed to say that I could not keep on carrying trees.

What?

What a weird thing to say.

I believe that the Lord was referring to family trees.

When we pray for someone, whether we know it or not, we are also praying for the person's family.

As you may have noticed, we do not live in isolation.

Our family of origin is always "with" us in some sense.

Jesus carried THE TREE, the CROSS.

Jesus did it.

Lord Jesus, I entrust these concerns to YOU! You won the victory for us on THE TREE, the CROSS.

## FAINTING DURING A HOMILY

After seminary graduation, over thirty years ago, I was invited to preach in an Episcopal church a couple of hours away.

The rector of the parish was away and a parishioner would be there to officiate at Morning Prayer. The choir would be present. The congregation would be there.

During the homily, I realized something serious was happening.

A parishioner had collapsed!

Midge, from the choir, was immediately there beside the lady who had fainted. Midge is a nurse and carried nitroglycerin.

The lady revived and then the paramedics were there to check on her. The church and the town are both small and it is a mercy that the paramedics could be there so soon.

When Midge was there with the lady, I started to leave the pulpit to be with the lady who had fainted, but the congregation motioned me to stay in the pulpit and PRAY! I did so.

Humorously, the sound system was working really well. Terry had rewired the church so those who had trouble hearing could hear better.

As I prayed, in a fairly soft voice, the sound system seemed to reverberate with "LORD, WE PRAY ALSO FOR THESE PARAMEDICS …."

Anyway, that Sunday quite an experience in several ways.

There was a visiting Lutheran who came up to me at the coffee hour, after the service, and said thank you. She said something in my homily had helped her clear up a theological problem she had been having.

You never know!

Every day we just show up and do what the Lord tells us.

Once in a while, there is quite an adventure!

## YOU ARE IN THE FAMILY!

There was a recent fund drive for my favorite radio station.

It was announced that when you sent in your donation you were part of the "family."

That's great!

I really like this station and am happy to send in a donation.

However, when it comes to God's family, I don't have to send in a donation.

Jesus sent in a donation for me.

Jesus paid the price.

He shed His Precious Blood on the Cross.

Jesus gave HIMSELF on the Cross so that I could be part of God's family.

## YOUR CREDIT SCORE

Do you HAVE to get acknowledgement for what you do?

Do you HAVE to get thanked for what you do?

Do you HAVE to be right?

Do you go crazy when someone else gets the credit for what you did?

Not to worry!

The Lord will give you an even bigger reward that you can imagine.

Relax.

## THE SADDEST VERSE

What do you think is the saddest verse in the Gospel of John?

Do you think it was it was when the crucified Jesus cried out, "It is finished (John 19, 30)?"

No, that was a cry of victory!

Jesus had completed the great work of redemption on our behalf.

To me, the saddest verse in the Gospel of John is in the majestic Prologue of the Gospel.

"He came unto his own, and his own received him not (John 1, 11 KJV)."

This is a verse to remember when we feel misunderstood and forgotten.

St. Paul, you remember, referred to sharing in the sufferings of Christ.

"I want to know Christ and the power of his resurrection and the sharing of his sufferings by becoming like him in his death, if somehow I may attain the resurrection from the dead (Philippians 3, 10-11, NRSV)."

## CONCEALED

Answered.

Concealed.

Concealed in a storm cloud.

Psalm 81 tells of calling out to God in distress.

God answered and rescued.

However, God answered in an unusual way.

Concealed.

God answered, concealed in a storm cloud.

## REAPPRAISAL

The apostle Paul reappraised as loss the very things he used to consider as gain.

Light.

The light of Christ.

Within dazzling light of Christ, Paul reappraised these things.

## FEAR AND COMPLAINING

Read the book of Exodus.

## SACRIFICES

My favorite book by Louisa May Alcott is <u>Eight Cousins</u>.

The young Rose, an orphan, asks her Uncle Alec, a physician, who is now her guardian, the following question. "People who make sacrifices are very much loved and admired, aren't they?"

Uncle Alec wisely replied, "If the sacrifice is a true one. But many of the bravest are never known, and get no praise.

## THE SOULS ENTRUSTED TO YOUR CARE

Here is bit of wisdom, also from <u>Eight Cousins</u>. This is another insight from Dr. Alex.

The doctor noted that parents often were so absorbed in their work that they tended not to "…study their children, and cherish that sweet and natural confidence which is a child's surest safeguard, and a parent's subtlest power. Happy the boys and girls who tell all things freely to father and mother, sure of pity, help, and pardon; and thrice happy the parents who, out of their own experience, and by their own virtues, can teach and uplift the souls for which they are responsible."

This book was published in 1874. We absolutely need to hear this in our present culture.

## THE PAUSE BUTTON

This is Lent, 2020.

The corona virus.

Everything is changed.

Lord, help us.

Thank you for transforming us during this unexpected retreat.

## CLASS DISMISSED!

What happens when the teacher says, "Class dismissed?"

The students are eager to go free!

So, what happens when we read in Philippians 4, 6-7 that WE are the ones to dismiss all anxiety?

Our worries go and we are free to take a deep breath and to resume living!

## SPICE OR STAFF?

Variety is not only the spice of life.

Variety is also a necessity, truly a staff of life, to keep us going forward.

## WHEN TERRY INTEGRATED THE OLD ORIGINAL

The Old Original was the name of the Mexican restaurant of Terry's father. Terry and his brothers Barry and Randall grew up helping in the restaurant.

Once, when Terry was in high school, he was left in charge while his father was briefly away. A group of soldiers from nearby Fort Hood came into the Old Original to have lunch.

This was during the time of racial segregation and one of the soldiers was African American. One of the workers asked Terry what to do.

Without hesitation, Terry said to seat all the soldiers and to serve them lunch.

## ARA AND THE OWL

One of the funniest time Ara, now two years old, and I have had was when she was a little younger. Christopher and Zuli and Ara were here to visit. We discovered a stuffed toy owl and had fun tossing it into the air and saying, "Uh oh!" Ara would giggle and we would look to see where the owl had "flown" and then retrieve it and do this all over.

## BACK TO SCHOOL

This is a refresher course! It is January, 2022. We just had groceries delivered.

It had been fun, for a while, to go again to my favorite store, walk right in, get a gift card, say hello to a favorite checker, and go on home.

Well, right now, we are again advised to be very careful about going out.

This corresponds with my increased sense of the Lord calling me to greater silence.

Lord Jesus, we pray for our poor country, our poor world, our Church. We are all in need of your instructions on how to live in this time.

We look to YOU!

We place all our trust in YOU!

You alone have the final word about what is happening in our lives, our Church, our country, and our world. ALLELUIA!

## I DON'T WANT TO LEAVE THIS WORLD WITHOUT MEETING MYSELF

We spend so much time meeting others' expectations or trying to meet what we think are others' expectations.

I am going to spend this Lent another way.

## SUNRISE AND WISTERIA!

The film, "Enchanted April" begins with an advertisement in the newspaper. It was a dreary cold, foggy day in London. The words in the ad were "Sunshine and Wisteria."

This morning, March 3, 2022, I was overwhelmed with the beauty of a gentle, yet dazzling, sunrise. I watched from the living room and then opened the door to the deck. The deck was drenched from last night's rain, but the sunrise was blazingly bright. Overwhelmed, I watched and felt like a child, clapping her hands, applauding the Creator of such beauty.

I am now in my study to begin work on this manuscript.

Guess what! Outside my study window, the wisteria is just starting to BLOOM!

Glory!

### EASTER ENERGY

This morning, even within the octave of Easter, I was feeling tired.

I noticed, in our email, the video for today, April 23, 2022, of Fr. Mark Goring, a young Canadian priest from St. Mary's Church, Ottawa. The title is "How to Renew Your Strength." Just what I needed.

It was a short video (less than two minutes) but gave the recommendation for the book called I THIRST (about Mother Teresa) and the verses from Isaiah about renewing our strength. Just what I needed!

"Even youths will faint and be weary, and the young will fall exhausted; but those who wait for the LORD shall renew their strength, they shall mount up with wings like eagles, they shall run and not be weary, they shall walk and not faint." (Isaiah 40, 30-31 NRSV).

Thank you, LORD, for this encouragement. ALLELUIA!

### GALLEY SLAVES ARE ROWING YOU TO YOUR DESTINY!

On August 15, 1992, the Assumption of the Blessed Virgin Mary, I began to read <u>Abandonment to Divine Providence</u> by Jean-Pierre de Caussade, a French Jesuit priest (1675-1751). My copy is a Doubleday Image Book, translated by John Beevers.

If you suffer because of people who do not wish you well, you will take great interest and comfort in Chapter VI, "All will be well if we abandon ourselves to God." It is in Part 6, "An abandoned soul is not afraid of its enemies, but finds them useful allies."

"God makes the soul take such suitable measures that they completely confound those who seek to trap it. Their stratagems bring it into its harbor like galley slaves rowing all out."

## HINGES

I asked Terry if a door with a door knob could be made to open either way. He said, "Yes, if it has the right hinges."

In the Catholic Church, there are cardinals.

They are truly "hinges."

They serve as hinges.

"Cardinalis." "Cardin-." "Cardo."

When you look up "cardinal" in the MERRIAM-WEBSTER'S COLLEGIATE DICTIONARY, Eleventh Edition, you will find these fascinating words.

Cardinals are "hinges."

## A WALK AROUND A BLOCK

This was a crazy week!

Finally, late Friday afternoon, I made a cup of coffee in the beautiful Notre Dame coffee mug Terry gave me and decided to take a walk around the block.

Saw a neighbor with three adorable granddaughters. One has decided to become a professional baseball player.

Saw Jennie, whom I don't really know, but met once, and her husband, and admired her lovely purple daisies. Would like to get Terry to meet her husband, also an engineer.

Then saw a couple, also walking, and noticed the woman was wearing a red Cornell t-shirt. Had to tell her about my professor daughter-in-law who went from Canada to Cornell for college, then on to Caltech for her doctorate.

Then, at a house where I don't know anyone, there was a big box of oranges being given away with bags provided! I took five, one of each of us in case we get to see Chris and Zuli and Ara soon. Went to the porch to say thank you and talked with the owner. She was ever so kind.

Then, when I was about home, I noticed the house across the street with the door open. The owner was in Paris, so I was concerned. Stood in the street and decided to go over and yell out, "If you are a burglar, come out of here!" If someone came out, what would I do? Throw oranges at the burglar and call the police on my tiny flip phone? The villain came out and turned out to be another neighbor who was bringing in the mail!

This was a very healing walk.

## GATHERED

Quietly listening to a Fisherfolk album called "Love Divine," I was drawn to the closing words.

> "As grain, once scattered on the hillsides,
> Was in this broken bread made one,
> So from all lands thy Church be gather'd
> Into thy kingdom by Thy Son."

[ (<u>Rendez a Dieu</u> , Louis Bourgeois, 1543), Greek, from the <u>Didache</u>, c. 110; Translated by F. Bland Tucker, 1941].

## GUARD, GATEKEEPER, OR GREETER

When we strive to enter some places, we encounter guards. They want to check our credentials. They may refuse entry.

When we enter other places, we encounter gatekeepers. As with guards, the are there to control our access. They also may refuse entry.

When we enter other places, we are greeted with kindness and genuine joy that we are there! At last. We are home.

## LAUGHTER!

I love Psalm 126. It is about redemption and restoration.

> "When the LORD restored the fortunes of Zion,
>     we were like those who dream.
> Then our mouth was filled with
>     laughter,
> And our tongue with shouts of
>     joy;
> then it was said among the
>     nations,
> 'The LORD has done great
>     things for them.'
> The LORD has done great things
>     for us
> and we rejoiced.
>
> Restore our fortunes, O LORD,
> like the watercourses in the
>     Negeb.
> May those who sow in tears
>     reap with shouts of joy.
> Those who go out weeping,
>   bearing their seeds for sowing,
>   shall come home with shouts of

> joy,
> carrying their sheaves." (NRSV)

God laughs and so should we!

## GOD WINS!

Once, when Christopher was about ten or twelve, I asked him about the book of the Revelation. He said, "It's simple. It means God wins."

> " 'Why do the nations conspire,
> and the peoples plot in vain?
> The kings of the earth set
> themselves,
> And the rulers take counsel
> together,
> Against the LORD and his
> anointed, saying,
> 'Let us burst their bonds asunder,
> and cast their cords from us.'
>
> He who sits in the heavens laughs;
> The LORD has them in derision.
> Then he will speak to them in his
> wrath,
> and terrify them in his fury,
> saying,
> 'I have set my king on Zion, my
> holy hill.'" (Psalm 2, 2-6 NRSV).
>
> "Happy are all who take refuge in
> Him." (Psalm 2, 12b NRSV)

So let us place all our trust in the LORD.

GOD WINS!

TO GOD BE ALL THE GLORY!

A.M.D.G.

You may order additional copies of this book

from www.amazon.com, www.barnesandnoble.com,

or through your favorite bookstore.

www.ingramcontent.com/pod-product-compliance
Lightning Source LLC
Chambersburg PA
CBHW031426040426
42444CB00006B/698